S0-BNB-057

HOLSTEIN
Large black-and-white dairy cattle. A breed that has been adapted to life on the pampas is called Holando Argentino.

ABERDEEN ANGUS
Aberdeen Angus are short, stocky beef cattle, usually all black. Neither the bulls nor the cows grow horns.

PELUDO
(pay-LOO-doh)
The peludo is a type of armadillo that has hair (pelo) growing between its scales. It eats insects and dead animals.

VENEZUELA
COLOMBIA
GUYANA
SURINAM
FRENCH GUYANA
ECUADOR
PERU
SOUTH AMERICA
BRAZIL
BOLIVIA
PARAGUAY
ATLANTIC OCEAN
PACIFIC OCEAN
CHILE
ARGENTINA
URUGUAY
THE PAMPAS
BUENOS AIRES
MY MAMA'S RANCH

LA LUZ MALA
(Lah LOOS MAH-lah)
A flamelike glow that sometimes hovers over the ground at night, especially where there are skeletons of cows, horses, or other animals. It is caused by a chemical reaction between the animal bones and the soil.

GALLARETA
(gah-yah-RAY-ta)
A water bird, similar to a duck, that is very common on the pampas.

GAUCHO CLOTHES

RASTRA
(RAH-stra)
A gaucho belt made from a wide strip of leather decorated with silver coins, usually from different countries. Some gauchos have their initials on the buckle.

BOMBACHA
(bome-BAH-cha)
Loose gaucho pants.

CRIOLLO HORSE
(cree-OH-yo) Horse
The criollo horse is a sturdy, good-looking horse descended from Spanish and Arabian horses.

ALPARGATAS
(ahl-par-GAH-tahs)
Rope-soled canvas shoes.

To my mother and to my nieces, Eugenia and Laura.
—M.C.B.

Henry Holt and Company, Inc.
Publishers since 1866
115 West 18th Street
New York, New York 10011

Henry Holt is a registered
trademark of Henry Holt and Company, Inc.

Published in Canada by Fitzhenry & Whiteside Ltd.,
195 Allstate Parkway, Markham, Ontario L3R 4T8.

Library of Congress Cataloging-in-Publication Data
Brusca, María Cristina.
My mama's little ranch on the pampas / María Cristina Brusca.
Sequel to: On the pampas. c1991.
1. Pampas (Argentina)—Description and travel—Juvenile
literature.   2. Gauchos—Argentina—Juvenile literature.
3. Ranch life—Argentina—Juvenile literature.   I. Title.
F2926.B77   1994   982—dc20   93-28113

ISBN 0-8050-2782-3

First Edition—1994

Printed in the United States of America
on acid-free paper. ∞

1   3   5   7   9   10   8   6   4   2

MY MAMA'S LITTLE RANCH
ON THE PAMPAS

María Cristina Brusca

Reinoso   Mingo   M. Cristina   Guillermo   Mama   Papa
Pampero

Henry Holt and Company
New York

One steamy afternoon in January, my brother Guillermo
and I were helping mend the fences at my mother's
new ranch. "Okay, more wire now," called out Reinoso, the
gaucho who worked for Mama.

Our neighbor Mingo rode by on his horse and waved. "Fix
those fences good!" he said, laughing. "No beef cattle
allowed on my dairy farm!" We had to fix all our fences
before Mama could buy cows and put them in our pasture.

It had only been a couple of weeks since Mama bought her very own ranch. I remember the day we all came from Buenos Aires, the city where we lived, to see it for the first time.

Mama, Papa, Guillermo, and I drove for five hours to get to the little ranch, and the last fifty kilometers were over bumpy, dusty dirt roads. Mama's ranch was much smaller than *La Carlota,* our grandparents' ranch, but to Guillermo and me it was the most wonderful place in the world.

There was a little house, a corral, two windmills, a ragged old barn, and an electric generator that rarely worked, and was noisy when it did.

My father had to go back to the city to work, but he came out to the farm every weekend. Mama, Guillermo, and I were going to stay there all summer.

Mingo lent us a milk cow, and my mother milked her every morning. In the evening, Guillermo and I put her into the corral, away from her calf, so she'd have milk the next day.

We had other chores too: we fed the pigs, and every morning we opened the windmill so its blades would turn and pump water out of the ground for the animals. In the evening we would shut it off again. That was hard work, like fighting the wind!

One day, Salguero, a gaucho from my grandparents' ranch, rode over to our farm with my horse Pampero. The summer before, I had trained Pampero to come when I rattled a bucket of corn. He hadn't forgotten, and he'd still come galloping to me, in smaller and smaller circles, until finally he'd rest his head on my shoulder and eat his favorite treat.

Guillermo rode Mingo's red pony, but he longed for a sturdy *criollo* horse like his hero Reinoso's. Guillermo followed the gaucho everywhere, imitating the way he walked and talked, and asking about his past as a famous horse breaker.

Finally we finished mending the fences. Now my mother could buy some cows. So one morning in February, my parents took us to the cattle auction. Even before we got there we could hear the mooing of hundreds of cattle, the stomping of their hooves, and the shouts of the gauchos. We could smell the cattle and the stinging odor of manure in the summer heat.

The auctioneer, Don Angel Santos Ruffo, rode around on a funny-looking cart with a high platform from which he could see and be seen by everybody at the auction. He stopped at each corral to auction off the cattle.

"These are the ones I want," said Mama, showing us a herd of beautiful young black Aberdeen Angus.

We waited beside their corral for Don Angel to drive up. "Look at these fine heifers from *Estancia Los Peludos*!" he began. Mama was ready. "Two years old, and every one of them pregnant," continued the auctioneer. "Do I hear thirty *pesos* a head?" My mother lifted one finger and offered twenty. The auctioneer nodded at her. "Twenty-one," offered somebody else, and he nodded again. "Twenty-two!" "Twenty-four!" "Twenty-six!" "Going once, going twice, *sold*!" My mother had bought the cows, and at a very good price.

That afternoon, Guillermo and I opened the gates. With a thundering of hooves, Mama's new cows were driven into our pasture. Now we'd see how our fences would hold up!

Early the next Saturday, we gathered the cows together to brand them with a mark we'd designed ourselves. Like a real gaucho, yelling and pushing the cattle with my horse, I drove them into the chute. My mother heated the branding iron over a fire, and Reinoso branded the cattle. Guillermo handed the vaccines to my father, who gave each cow a shot.

By the time we finished, the sun was setting. We ate a big *asado* and the traditional branding-day *pasteles*.

The summer passed too quickly, and before we knew it, it was March, time for Guillermo and me to go back to school. My brother packed up his insect collection, his ovenbird nest, and his cow skull. I took Pampero for a last gallop out to the far pasture, then hugged him good-bye. We'd be coming back for weekends, but it wouldn't be the same. Reinoso would stay and take care of the ranch for us, and sometimes my mother would be there too, while the rest of us were in the city.

Three whole weeks went by before Guillermo and I returned to the ranch. The weather was already getting cool. The cows, who were going to have their calves in July or August, looked fatter.

"Let's check the fences," suggested my brother. He ran to get Reinoso's tools, and we rode slowly along the edges of the ranch. Suddenly I noticed one of our cows tangled in the wire on Mingo's side of the fence. She was a little cow, not as fat as the others, with a white star on her forehead.

Her foot was cut, and she had a rebellious look in her eye. Trying to stay out of the way of her kicking hooves, Guillermo quickly put some ointment on her foot, the way Reinoso had taught him, and we cut the barbed wire. As soon as she was free, she ran back to her own pasture.

I told Mama about the little cow, and she said, "Oh, that naughty girl! She's been over at Mingo's at least five times this month!"

By April, the weather was very chilly. My mother bought a sulky and a white mare named Rosa, and taught me to harness and drive her. We practiced driving around the ranch, checking on all the cows with their big bellies. Only our friend the little cow with the white star didn't look pregnant.

For my birthday in May, my parents let me drive the sulky into town with Guillermo. After we'd gone to the butcher shop and the bakery, we ventured into the general store *"La Puñalada."* It got its name, "The Stab," long ago when a gaucho was stabbed to death there! There was even a big picture of a knife fight on the wall. The owner was playing music on an old Victrola, and my brother and I danced the *malambo,* much to the amusement of the gauchos.

In July, we had our winter vacation, and we went to the ranch for two whole weeks. It was raining a lot that winter, and our car got stuck in the mud. Luckily, a friendly gaucho came by and pulled us out with his horse.

It rained all the first week. Once a day one of us rode out to check the cows. When it was Mama's turn, she had a better idea: she watched them from the house, through a pair of binoculars!

Guillermo and I spent a lot of time in the barn, learning to take care of our reins and saddles, and even to braid our own harnesses. Reinoso told wonderful stories, and we listened, drinking *mate* and eating *tortas negras*. I showed Reinoso the real gaucho belt my grandparents had given me, and he admired it.

One afternoon my mother burst into the barn, waving her binoculars. "We have our first calf!" she announced.

Soon there were many more baby calves. The rain stopped and the sky cleared, so we spent the rest of our vacation in the fields. By the time we had to go back to school, about half of the cows had little wobbly calves next to them.

Spring begins on September twenty-first, and by October, it was getting nice and warm. Because of the rainy winter, the far pasture was flooded. Many water birds—ducks, *gallaretas,* white egrets, sea gulls, and even flamingos— had built their nests there.

"Let's make an egg collection," proposed Guillermo. "If we take one egg from each nest, the birds won't even notice." But they *did* notice! Just as I was reaching for the first egg, *splat!* Bird droppings came raining down on our heads. Hundreds of sea gulls were circling above us, and all together, as though on cue, they bombed us with yucky white splatter. Their defense worked too. We never did finish that egg collection.

In November, the grass was greener, and everywhere we looked there were calves nursing. The only cow without a calf was our friend with the star on her forehead. But now *she* looked fat. Maybe she'd have a calf after all.

School ended on the last day of November. On our first night back at the ranch we went out hunting for *peludos* with Reinoso. Every time we saw one of the little armadillos, we would throw ourselves off our horses and try to grab it before it scurried off into its cave. We rode so far that we couldn't see our house or even our windmill.

Suddenly Reinoso gasped, *"La luz mala!"* Just ahead of us an eerie glow hovered over the ground. "The ghost of Santos Vega!" cried Reinoso, wheeling his horse around. My heart jumped. I spurred Pampero and didn't look back until I was safely home. I shuddered to think I'd almost met the ghost of Santos Vega, the gaucho who'd lost his soul to the devil in a guitar-playing match!

One evening, just a few days before Christmas, when I was riding back to the house, I noticed that the little cow seemed to be in trouble. I took her back to the corral and called Mama and Guillermo. Reinoso was visiting his family, and Papa was still in the city.

"Her calf is about to be born," said Mama, "but something's wrong. Look, those are its feet, so it's positioned okay," she explained. "Maybe it's too big for her. I don't want to pull it out—we might hurt her. We'd better call the vet."

There wasn't a phone or a car at the ranch. So I raced across the fields to ask Mingo to drive into town for the vet. Then I galloped home as fast as I could.

Mingo soon roared up in his truck, parking with its headlights shining on the corral, and Dr. López, the veterinarian, jumped out.

"There's just one way to save her life," he said after examining the cow, "and I'm not sure I can save the calf. She needs a cesarean operation: I'll cut her open to take the calf out. And I'm going to need some help."

He gave the cow a shot, so she wouldn't feel any pain. Right away she got groggy, and Mingo, my mother, and the vet helped her lie down.

"Now you can help," he said to me. "Put your knee on her neck so she'll keep still. And Guillermo, there's going to be blood. Take this cloth and keep her clean."

Then the vet cut the cow's belly. We watched, amazed, as he reached in and pulled out a great big calf by its feet. The calf didn't move. "Is it dead?" asked Guillermo.

"I don't know," said the vet, who was already sewing the cow up. "Dry the calf off. And you, Mingo, massage its throat, and we'll see."

Suddenly the calf's mouth moved and one eye opened. It was alive!

"Wow!" whispered my brother, awed, and Mama hugged me, and there were even tears in Mingo's eyes.

And the cow, who was already standing up, licked her calf. The vet gave her a big dose of antibiotics so she wouldn't get an infection, and said she'd heal in no time. She was already able to nurse the calf.

The calf was very large, with black-and-white spots. "I know who *your* father is," said Mingo. "My holstein bull!" Holsteins are much larger than Aberdeen Angus, and this calf was big like her father—too big for her little Angus mother.

The next day was Christmas Eve. Even though it was very hot, we lit the wood oven and roasted a pig, and when Papa arrived from the city that night, we all sat down together for Christmas Eve dinner. At exactly midnight, we toasted to welcome Christmas Day. Then we opened our presents.

Guillermo and I brought the calf into the garden to show my father. We named her *Manchita,* which means "Spot," and fed her some extra milk, because her mother didn't have enough.

It was very late, but before I went to bed, I got some corn
and walked out to the fields to visit my horse. The warm,
gentle breeze smelled wonderful. And since the generator
had broken down again, it was dark and quiet and peaceful.
I could hear the cattle in the fields and a train passing in the
distance.

I rattled the corn in the bucket, and Pampero came
galloping to me and put his head on my shoulder. As he
crunched his corn, I looked up at the stars and thought
about all the funny and scary and wonderful things that had
happened that first year at my mother's beautiful ranch.

THE SEASONS

SPRING IN THE NORTH
FALL IN THE SOUTH

WINTER IN THE NORTH
SUMMER IN THE SOUTH

SUMMER IN THE NORTH
WINTER IN THE SOUTH

FALL IN THE NORTH
SPRING IN THE SOUTH

The Earth travels around the sun once a year, and rotates on its axis once a day. Because this axis is at a permanent angle, the North Pole tilts toward the sun during one half of the year, and the South Pole during the other half.

When the North Pole faces the sun, the Northern Hemisphere warms up. While North America enjoys summer, it is winter in Argentina and other parts of the Southern Hemisphere.

When the South Pole faces the sun, warmth comes to the Southern Hemisphere. So in December, during the North American winter, it is summer in Argentina.

MATE
(MAH-tay)
Mate is a very bitter, greenish hot drink similar to tea. It is sipped through a metal straw, called a bombilla *(bome-BEE-yah), from a hollow gourd that is passed around.*

TORTAS NEGRAS
(TOR-tahs NAY-grahs)
Tortas ("cakes") negras ("black") are baked in the oven and look like flat biscuits with burnt brown sugar on top.

PASTELES
(pah-STAY-lays)
Pasteles are fried pastries filled with thick quince or sweet potato jam.

MALAMBO
(mah-LAHM-bo)
The malambo is a dance performed only by men. To a rapid drumbeat, a dancer stamps, alternating heels and toes, crossing and uncrossing his feet, and sometimes springing into the air.

SPANISH NAMES

MANCHITA
(mahn-CHEE-tah)
REINOSO (ray-NO-so)
MINGO (MEENG-go)

GUILLERMO
(ghee-YAIR-mo)

SALGUERO (sahl-GAY-roh)
LA CARLOTA (lah car-LOH-tah)
SANTOS VEGA (SAHN-tohs VAY)

PAMPERO
(pahm-PAY-roh)

DON ANGEL SANTOS RUFFO
(dawn AHN-hel SAHN-tos ROO)
ESTANCIA LA CARLOTA
(es-TAHN-see-ah lah car-LOH-t)

ASADO
(ah-SAH-doh)
Meat, usually beef, roasted slowly outdoors over a fire.